Kirsty Seymour-Ure

KITTEN@PLAY

RYLAND
PETERS
& SMALL

London   New York

Senior Designer Paul Tilby
Editor Miriam Hyslop
Location Research Manager Kate Brunt
Production Patricia Harrington
Art Director Gabriella Le Grazie
Publishing Director Alison Starling

First published in the United Kingdom in 2002
by Ryland Peters & Small
12–14 Whitfield Street, Kirkman House,
London W1T 2RP
www.rylandpeters.com

10 9 8 7 6 5 4 3 2 1

Text, design and photographs
© Ryland Peters & Small 2002

Printed and bound in China

ISBN 1 84172 284 7

contents

purrfect pets

So bright and full of life, so tiny and yet so bold, with that winning mix of impertinence and innocence, kittens are the most enchanting of little creatures.

All kittens are fluffy. But long-haired kittens are really a ball of soft, soft wool. You may sometimes be caught out by a gleam of eyes from deep within a fluffy face. Picking up that soft ball of fur, you feel the quick beating of the heart against your fingers.

FLUFFIER, FLUFFIEST

Utterly vulnerable at their birth, in a couple of weeks kittens will have fizzed to life. Eyes wide open and often strikingly blue (a colour that usually changes), they begin to explore their new world, tentatively and then with increasing boldness. Shaky on their legs as they may be, from the very

EARLY DAYS

first they demonstrate the curiosity for which they are justly notorious. Their dexterity does not yet match their desire to investigate, and young kittens in a litter spend much time scrambling all over each other and not getting very far in any direction.

Having no reason not to be, kittens are usually sweet-natured; but from a young age they all manifest different personality traits. Like humans, some kittens are timid or stand-off-ish, others enjoy cuddles, some are truly courageous, while many are downright foolhardy. Most exhibit a mixture of characteristics, but nearly all  seem to be bright and cheerful. Stroke a kitten gently with your finger and wait for the purring to begin: a tiny motor thrumming away inside an equally tiny body. A kitten's purr, coming and going as if it is still at the practice stage, seems not quite real, and all the more special for that.

15

The combination of so tiny a face and such enormous ears must be one of a kitten's most winsome aspects. The disproportion can be so great that sometimes a kitten will even resemble an (exceptionally pretty) bat. The ears are immensely eloquent, flickering this way and that to pick up

FINEST FEATURES

the smallest sound, flattened right back in fear or anger, or pricking up with kittenish interest. They are beautiful, too: delicate, thin, almost transparent, so that light glows through them.

setting forth

Their size belies their courage and audacity: diminutive as they may be, kittens are lions at heart. Almost as soon as they can walk, they are out stalking.

They may think that they are fearless, but in truth kittens are easily startled and can be shy and clingy. You cannot predict them, however: whether they

LET ME AT HIM

will stand up to the enormous dog and flee the coffee grinder, or vice versa, is simply impossible to judge. Kittens have a crazy streak in them just waiting to be set free.

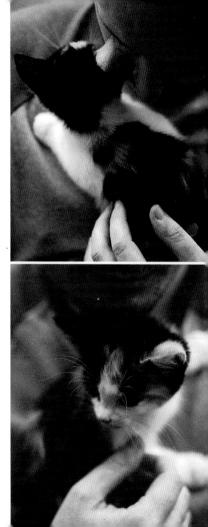

TESTING THE GROUND

They bound forth boldly and then they screech to a halt. Coat bristling, tail fluffed out, ears flattened back and tiny sharp teeth bared, they emit an experimental snarl. What do they see? We never find out, for onward they run again on their gleeful path, intrepid, carefree and cheerfully oblivious to

any real danger.

Kittens are born with an unstoppable urge to go out and explore. Hardly are their eyes open than they are taking little staggering steps away from the mother, sallying forth into the great wide unknown world impelled by the

TAILS OF ADVENTURE

innate feline need to find out what is going on just round the next corner, behind that flowerpot, or up on those shelves. Kittens adore wriggling into and out of small dark holes and narrow spaces; cardboard boxes provide them with hours of fun leaping in, leaping out, running round in circles inside and out, leaping in, leaping out...

A-HUNTING I WILL GO

In these early days hunting is not much different from exploring for a kitten. She will pounce on anything that attracts her, be it a falling leaf, a piece of string or her own tail. At this stage mice need have no worries.

28

feline friends

Naturally friendly and sociable, kittens thrive in company. Playing is so much more fun, and the potential for a bit of mischief so much greater when in a group.

Born into a litter of six or so, a kitten rarely lacks company in its first couple of months of life. Unlike dogs, cats are not pack animals, but the solitary nature of the cat seems not to inhibit the kitten's amicable character. Kittens in a litter sleep curled up together in a soft tangle of legs and tails, surely comforted by the warm presence of their brothers and sisters. A kitten on your lap will rub its cheek against your hand in the instinctual gesture of ownership, and will arch its back to be stroked. This, for a cat, is a close thing to love.

ME AND MY KITTEN

It has to be said, kittens and children don't always get on. A kitten's tail is so enticingly pullable, a child's face so scratchable. Children love kittens, but kittens are wise to reserve judgment.

A kitten sits neatly in a grown adult person's hand and furthermore is just the right size to put in your pocket. Some unusually sociable kittens love being carried about like this, being taken to interesting, un-catlike places and developing an ever-widening circle of human friends and acquaintances.

A kitten can turn from the quietest, sweetest, most laid-back bundle of purring fur into a hissing, spitting, writhing creature with wild eyes and thrashing tail virtually at the touch of a button. But which button? Perhaps one starts to tease the other during a mutual grooming session, which then

turns violent; or one kitten simply feels like a bit of action and cuffs the other round the head with a well-aimed paw. Tussling involves much noise and fuss but merely cements the friendship. No hard feelings.

fun and games

Playing is what kittens are best at. Their high spirits, their agility and strength, their curiosity and dauntlessness – all combine to form the perfect play machine.

It might be work for some people, but for kittens it's a thoughtfully provided playscheme. Kittens, of course, don't distinguish work from play. To them, all work is play, all play is work, and all the objects on your well-equipped desk were chosen solely for their benefit.

IN A TANGLE

A tangle of twine can keep a kitten enjoyably entertained for hours. With a concentration as comical as it is intense, they try out the repertoire of moves that will later allow them to stalk real rather than pretend prey. Right now, a twist of string can be more dangerous than the real thing.

Kittens treat the whole world as their private adventure playground, expressly designed for them to play the endless games that serve to develop their feline skills. Their mother has shown them how to hunt; how to toss a mouse in the air and bat it about with gratuitous cruelty; how to close in for the kill. Now, ferocious and intent – if not strictly accurate – they practise on bits of paper, twigs and small balls.

Flower arrangements may be a thing of the past once a kitten is in your home. Kittens like flowers: pretty, good to smell, intriguing to taste, and easy to rip apart. The petals are

FLOWERS

so deliciously fragile, the stems so amusingly springy, the leaves so obligingly yielding to the unsheathed, expert claw. Kittens are good at flowers.

catnapping

Kittens sleep a lot, on their own or in groups. They'll fall asleep in the midst of a game, snooze quietly after a meal, or doze off in your lap, purring softly.

Like cats, kittens spend many hours asleep. But in the case of kittens it is usually justified, given the amount of energy they expend on simply being a kitten. They'll curl up with their play-mates and indulge in some communal dozing, safe in the warmth of each other; or they're just as happy to

COLLECTIVE DREAM

sleep on their own. This is where they begin to hone the special cat skill of finding the best spot. A sunny window sill or the airing cupboard are old favourites, but don't neglect to check your saucepans, the washing machine and the back of the sock drawer.

When the going gets tough, the tough – fall asleep. Sometimes a game just becomes too much. The toy mouse bites back, the ping-pong ball is too bouncy, the piece of string gets longer and longer and tries to tie you in knots. Close your eyes. When you wake up, the world will be perfect again.

CREDITS

The publisher would like to thank everyone who allowed us to photograph their kittens:

Sally, Valeria, Alex and Nick, Michelle and Andrew Walker,

Stephen Collier,

Mrs Dabbs,

Michelle Robinson
(breeder) mrobinson@beullaga.demon.co.uk
t. 020 7424 9374,

Margaret Nightingale
(breeder) 'Hawdene Persians' t. 020 8529 5015,

Karen Plummer www.tonkinesecats.net,

Mrs S. Seedham
Simply British breeder of quality BSH kittens.

Special thanks to
Tom, The Cat Place,
6 Clifton Road, London W9 1SS
t. 020 7289 1000